# Socks!

Whether you are knitting them for yourself or a loved one, hand-knit socks are a special treat. From dress socks perfect for the office to bulky socks ideal for a lazy afternoon at home, we have selected a few of our favorite patterns to encourage your own love of sock knitting. Featuring 8 patterns for everyone in the family, this book will inspire you to grab your needles and a ball of luscious yarn and cast on for hours of knitting fun.

Happy knitting!

*Jennifer*

Editor-in-Chief
*Love of Knitting*

# Best of
# Love of knitting
## Socks

# Streamers Socks

*Streamers are the quintessential party decoration, so what better accent to have on a delightful pair of holiday socks? Instantly feel holiday cheer every time you wear them. Yarn: Petals Sock by Universal Yarn/Debbie Macomber Blossom Street Collection*

**Designed by Kristin Hansen**

**Skill level:** Intermediate ● ● ● ○

**Sizes:** Women's Narrow (Women's Medium/Men's Narrow, Women's Wide/ Men's Medium, Men's Wide)

**Finished measurements:**
Approx 7 (8, 9, 10)" circumference

**Yarn weight:**

fine merino, 20% angora, 30% nylon, (462 yds/100g) in Plum Tree 605

- Two U.S. size 2 (2.75mm) 16" or 20" circular needles, or size required for gauge
- Waste yarn
- Yarn needle

## Gauge
28 sts and 32 rows = 4" (10cm) in St st

## Materials
- 1 skein Petals Sock by Universal Yarn/Debbie Macomber Blossom Street Collection, 50% superwash

## Special abbreviations
T2F: Purl the 2nd st through the back loop. Do not remove from left needle. Knit the first st. Slip both sts off needle.

T2B: Knit the 2nd st. Do not remove from left needle. Purl the first st. Slip both sts off needle.

## Stitch pattern

### Streamers

Rnd 1: *T2F, p6; rep from * around.

Rnd 2: *P1, T2F, p5; rep from * around.

Rnd 3: *P2, T2F, p4; rep from * around.

Rnd 4: *P3, T2F, p3; rep from * around.

Rnd 5: *P4, T2F, p2; rep from * around.

Rnd 6: *P5, T2F, p1; rep from * around.

Rnd 7: *P6, T2F; rep from * around.

Rnd 8: *P7, k1; rep from * around.

Rnd 9: *P6, T2B; rep from * around.

Rnd 10: *P5, T2B, p1; rep from * around.

Rnd 11: *P4, T2B, p2; rep from * around.

Rnd 12: *P3, T2B, p3; rep from * around.

Rnd 13: *P2, T2B, p4; rep from * around.

Rnd 14: *P1, T2B, p5; rep from * around.

Rnd 15: *T2B, p6; rep from * around.

Rnd 16: *K1, p7; rep from * around.

Rep rnds 1–16 for pat.

## Sock

### Cuff

Cast on 56 (64, 72, 80) sts. Divide sts evenly between 2 circular needles and join in a rnd. Work in k1, p1 rib for 10 rnds.

Set up rnd: *K1, p7; rep from * around. Work in streamers pat until leg measures approx 6¾" or desired length.

### Afterthought heel set up

Work in pat as set on needle 1 (instep sts). With waste yarn, knit sts on needle 2 (heel sts). Cut waste yarn, leaving a 3" tail on each end. Slide sts back to beg of needle 2 and knit in project yarn.

### Foot

Work even in pat on needle 1 and in St st on needle 2 until foot measures approx 2" less than desired length.

### Star toe

Rnd 1: Knit.

Rnd 2: *K12 (14, 16, 18); k2tog; rep from * around.

Rep rnds 1 and 2, working 1 less st each time before dec, until 12 (14, 16, 18) sts rem on each needle. Rep rnd 2 only until 4 sts rem on each needle. Cut yarn, leaving a 6" tail. Draw through rem sts, pull tight, and secure.

## Afterthought heel

Remove waste yarn, place heel sts evenly on needles 1 and 2; 28 (32, 36, 40) sts each needle. Knit 1 rnd, picking up and knitting 1 st at each end of each needle; 30 (34, 38, 42) sts each needle.

Rnd 1: Knit.

Rnd 2: *K13 (15, 17, 19), k2tog; rep from * around.

Rep rnds 1 and 2, working 1 less st each time before dec, until 8 sts rem on each needle. Cut yarn. Graft sts using Kitchener st.

## Finishing

Weave in ends. ▣

# Lazy Weekend Socks

*Knitting worsted weight yarn on size 4 needles makes this pair the perfect introduction to sock knitting. Learning the basics of sock construction, from turning the heel to decreasing at the toe, will be a breeze. Your first pair will always be your favorite pair, and these comfortable socks are no exception. Yarn: Shepherd Worsted by Lorna's Laces*

**Designed by Lorna Miser**

**Skill level:** Intermediate ●●●○

**Sizes:** Women's 9½–12, Men's 8½–11

**Finished measurement:** 9½" circumference

**Yarn weight:**

## Materials

- Shepherd Worsted by Lorna's Laces, 100% superwash wool, (225 yds/113g) in following amounts/colors: 2 skeins multicolor (MC) (Shenanigans) and 1 skein solid color (CC) (Douglas Fir)

- U.S. size 4 (3.5mm) set of 4 DPNs or 29" circular, or size required for gauge

- Stitch markers

- Yarn needle

## Gauge

20 sts and 28 rows = 4" (10cm) in k2, p2 rib

## Note

Project can be knit using either DPNs or a long circular and the magic loop method.

## Sock

### Leg

With MC, cast on 48 sts. Divide sts evenly on 3 needles or arrange as for magic loop. Place marker and join, being careful not to twist the sts. Work in k2, p2 rib for 8". Knit first st of next rnd (to center the rib on the instep).

### Heel flap

Change to CC and turn work.

Row 1 (WS): Slip 1, purl across 23 sts.

Row 2: *Slip 1, k1; rep from * across.

Rep rows 1 and 2 for a total of 24 rows.

### Turn heel

Continue in CC.

Row 1 (RS): Sl 1, k13, ssk, k1, turn.

Row 2: Sl 1, p5, p2tog, p1, turn.

Row 3: Sl 1, k6, ssk, k1, turn.

Row 4: Sl 1, p7, p2tog, p1, turn.

Row 5: Sl 1, k8, ssk, k1, turn.

Cont as set until all sts have been worked, ending with a WS row; 14 sts.

### Gusset

Change to MC. With RS facing, knit across heel sts. Pick up and knit 12 sts along side of heel flap, place marker, work in rib pat as set across 24 instep sts, place marker, pick up and knit 12 sts along opposite side of heel flap; 62 sts. Knit 7 heel sts to get to new beg of rnd (at center of heel).

Rnd 1: Knit to 3 sts before marker, k2tog, k1, work in rib pat across instep, k1, ssk, knit to end of rnd.

Rnd 2: Knit to marker, work in rib pat across instep, knit to end of rnd. Rep rnds 1 and 2 until 48 sts remain.

### Foot

Work even as set until foot measures 8½" or 1½" less than desired length.

### Toe

Change to CC.

Rnd 1: *Knit to 3 sts before marker, k2tog, k1, slip marker, k1, ssk; rep from * once more, knit to end.

Rnd 2: Knit.

Rep rnds 1 and 2 until 16 sts remain. Graft toe using Kitchener st.

## Finishing

Weave in ends. ⊞

# Magic Loop

SPECIAL
*Technique*

*Follow our simple steps to knit your next work-in-the-round project on one long circular needle instead of DPNs.*

Using a circular needle (at least 29" long), cast on the desired number of stitches.

Slide stitches onto the cable portion of the needle (photo A).

Find center of stitches; bend cable and pull through, leaving an equal number of stitches on each side of the "magic loop."

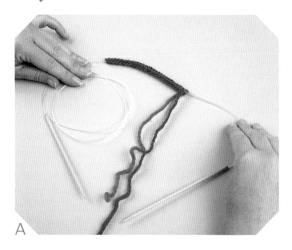

A

Slide each group of stitches onto the needle tips (photo B).

Hold needle tips in your left hand with the working yarn coming from the first stitch on the back needle.

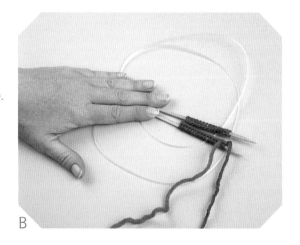

B

*Grab the back needle with your right hand, allowing the stitches on the back needle to slide back onto the cable (do not pull out the loop of cable) (photo C).

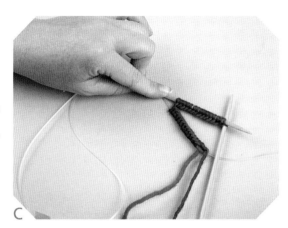

C

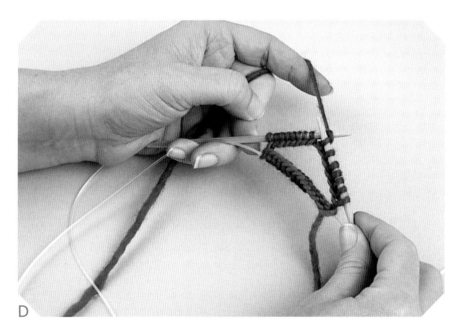

D

With the back needle, knit across the stitches on the front needle (photo D).

Turn needle so that the stitches just worked are on the back needle.

Push the stitches
that are on the
cable onto the
front needle

Repeat from *.

# Rattan Socks

*Soft merino socks are always a welcome addition, and these Rattan socks are no exception. The diamond pattern will delight sock knitters, keeping your fingers busy and engaged all of the way to the toes. Yarn: Baby Boom by Fiesta Yarns*

*The deeply textured stitch pattern looks great in solid yarns as well.*

**Designed by Kristin Hansen**

**Skill level:** Intermediate ●●●○

**Sizes:** Women's Narrow/Medium (Women's Wide/Men's Medium)

**Finished measurements:** Approx 7 (9)" circumference

**Yarn weight:**

## Materials

- 1 skein Baby Boom by Fiesta Yarns, 90% extra fine superwash merino, 10% nylon, (440 yds/100g) in color Camo Man

- Two U.S. size 2 (2.75mm) 20" circular needles (or set of 5 DPNs), or size required for gauge

- Cable needle

- Yarn needle

## Gauge

28 sts and 32 rows = 4" (10cm) in St st

## Special abbreviations

T2B: Slip 1 st to cable needle and hold in back, k1, p1 from cable needle.

T2F: Slip 1 st to cable needle and hold in front, p1, k1 from cable needle.

w&t (wrap and turn): Work to indicated st. Bring yarn between needles, slip next st purlwise, return yarn to original position and slip st back to left needle. Turn work.

## Stitch pattern

**Twist**

Rnd 1: K1, *p2, k2; rep from *, ending p2, k1.

Rnd 2: *K1, p1, T2B, T2F, p1, k1; rep from * around.

Rnd 3: *K1, p1, k1, p2, k1, p1, k1; rep from * around.

Rnd 4: *k1, T2B, p2, T2F, k1; rep from * around.

Rnd 5: K2, *p4, k4; rep from *, ending p4, k2.

Rnd 6: Knit.

Rnd 7: K1, *p2, k2; rep from *, ending p2, k1.

Rnd 8: *T2F, p1, k2, p1, T2B; rep from * around.

Rnd 9: *P1, k1, p1, k2, p1, k1, p1; rep from * around.

Rnd 10: *P1, T2F, k2, T2B, p1; rep from * to end of rnd.

Rnd 11: P2, *k4, p4; rep from *, ending k4, p2.

Rnd 12: Knit.

Rep rnds 1–12 for pat.

## Sock cuff

Cast on 48 (64) sts. Divide sts evenly over 2 circular needles (or 4 DPNs, if preferred). Work in k1 tbl, p1 rib for 10 rnds. Work in twist pat for approx 6½" or desired length, ending with rnd 6 or 12.

## Heel

Note: Work back and forth in rows on 24 (32) heel sts only; leave rem 24 (32) instep sts on hold.

Row 1 (WS): Purl to last 2 sts, w&t.

Row 2: Knit to last 2 sts, w&t.

Row 3: Purl to 1 st before last wrapped st, w&t.

Row 4: Knit to 1 st before last wrapped st, w&t.

Rep rows 3 and 4 until there are 8 unwrapped sts in center of heel. Complete heel as follows:

Row 1 (WS): Purl to first wrapped st, pick up wrap and purl tog with st, w&t next st (will have 2 wraps now on same st).

Row 2: Knit to first wrapped st, pick up wrap and knit tog with st, w&t next st (will have 2 wraps now on same st).

Row 3: Purl to first wrapped st, pick up both wraps and purl tog with st, w&t next st (will have 2 wraps now on same st).

Row 4: Knit to first wrapped st, pick up both wraps and knit tog with st, w&t

next st (will have 2 wraps now on same st). Rep rows 3 and 4 until all sts are worked.

## Foot

Resume working in the rnd. Work in twist pat over instep sts as set and St st over heel sts until foot measures approx 1¾" less than desired length.

## Toe

Rnd 1: Over instep sts, work k1, ssk, knit to last 3 sts, k2tog, k1; rep over heel sts; 4 sts dec.

Rnd 2: Knit.

Rep rnds 1 and 2 until 16 sts rem. Rep rnd 1 only until 8 sts rem. Graft toe closed using Kitchener st.

## Finishing

Weave in ends. ⊞

# Family of Socks

*This little sock went to market — and this family of foot warmers will too! Knit a pair for each family member. Socks are really "in" this year and are great fun to knit. Check out our "Special Technique: Grafting" on page 38, to make the toe finishing even easier.*

nylon (82 yds) in color 2302 Baby Blue

- Set of 4 size 1 (2.25 mm) double pointed needles

## Baby socks

Cast on 30 sts loosely.

Divide sts on 3 needles as follows:

Needle 1 (N1): 7 heel sts

Needle 2 (N2): 15 instep sts

Needle 3 (N3): 8 heel sts

Join and place a marker to indicate beg of round.

### Leg

Knit 21 rnds. On next round, complete sts on N2 and stop. (Leg should measure about 2½" from cast-on edge.)

### Heel flap

Slip N3 sts onto N1 (15 sts on needle).

Note: On first row only, k2, M1, complete row (16 sts).

On last row, decrease 1 st (15 sts remain).

With RS facing, work back and forth as follows:

Row 1: *Sl 1 purlwise, k1; repeat from * to end.

Row 2: Sl 1 purlwise, p to end.

# Baby Socks

**Skill level:** Intermediate ●●●○

**Size:** Infant shoe size 2

**Finished measurements:**
*Circumference of leg:* 4¼"
*Length of foot:* 3⅝"

**Yarn weight:**

## Gauge
28 sts and 35 rows = 4" (10 cm)

## Materials
- 1 ball Panda Cotton by Crystal Palace, 59% bamboo, 25% cotton, 16%

Repeat these 2 rows 7 more times (16 rows total).

## Turn heel

Note: Sl 1 = sl 1 purlwise.

Row 1 (RS): K9, ssk, k1. Turn.

Row 2 (WS): Sl 1, p4, p2tog, p1. Turn.

Row 3 (RS): Sl 1, k5, ssk, k1. Turn.

Row 4 (WS): Sl 1, p6, p2tog, p1. Turn.

Row 5 (RS): Sl 1, k7, ssk. Turn.

Row 6 (WS): Sl 1, p7, p2tog. Turn. (9 sts remain.)

Work 4 sts; place marker for beg of round.

## Heel gusset

With a free needle (N1), knit remaining 5 heel sts. Continuing with same needle, pick up 8 sts along the side of heel.

Pick up and knit 1 st from row below the first instep st to prevent a hole (14 sts on N1).

With a free needle (N2), work across 15 instep sts.

With free needle (N3), pick up and knit 1 st from row below first heel st to prevent a hole. With same needle, pick up 8 sts along side of heel and work across remaining heel sts (13 sts on N3).

## Shape gusset

Rnd 1 (dec rnd):

N1: Work to 3 sts from end; k2tog, k1.

N2: (Instep) Work even.

N3: K1, ssk, work to end.

Rnd 2: Work even.

Repeat rnds 1 and 2 until there are 30 sts remaining.

## Foot

Continue working in rnds until foot measures 2¾" from base of heel.

On next rnd, inc 2 sts — 1 st on N1 and 1 st on N2 — complete sts on N3. Place marker for beg of rnd.

## Shape toe

Rnd 1:

N1: (Sole) Work to last 3 sts, k2tog, k1.

N2: (Instep) K1, ssk, work to last 3 sts, k2tog, k1.

N3: (Sole) K1, ssk, complete round.

Rnd 2: Work even.

Repeat rnds 1 and 2 until 24 total sts remain.

Repeat rnd 1 until 12 sts remain (6 instep sts, 6 sole sts).

## Finishing

Work sts on N1. Slip sts from N3 to N1.

Holding N1 and N2 together, graft sts using Kitchener stitch (see grafting instructions on page 35).

Weave in ends.

# Toddler Socks

**Skill level:** Intermediate ●●●○

**Size:** Infant shoe size 8

**Finished measurements:**
*Circumference of leg:* 6"
*Length of foot:* 5½"
**Yarn weight:** 1

## Gauge

28 sts and 35 rows = 4" (10 cm)

## Materials

- 1 hank Fingering by Claudia Hand Painted Yarns, 100% Merino wool (175 yds/50g) in Purple Midnight
- Set of 4 size 2 (2.75 mm) double-pointed needles

## Toddler socks

Cast on 42 sts loosely.

Divide sts on 3 needles as follows:

Needle 1 (N1): 10 heel sts

Needle 2 (N2): 21 instep sts

Needle 3 (N3): 11 heel sts

Join and place a marker to indicate beg of round.

## Leg

Work in k1, p1 ribbing for 29 rnds. On next round, complete sts on N2 and stop. (Leg should measure about 3" from cast-on edge.)

## Heel flap

Slip N3 sts onto N1 (21 sts on needle).

Note: On first row only, k2, M1, complete row (22 sts).

On last row, decrease 1 st (21 sts remain).

With RS facing, work back and forth as follows:

Row 1: *Sl 1 purlwise, k1; repeat from * to end.

Row 2: Sl 1 purlwise, p to end.

Repeat these 2 rows 9 more times (20 rows total).

## Turn heel

Note: Sl 1 = sl 1 purlwise.

Row 1 (RS): K12, ssk, k1. Turn.

Row 2 (WS): Sl 1, p4, p2tog, p1. Turn

Row 3 (RS): Sl 1, k5, ssk, k1. Turn.

Row 4 (WS): Sl 1, p6, p2tog, p1. Turn.

Row 5 (RS): Sl 1, k7, ssk, k1. Turn.

Row 6: (WS) Sl 1, p8, p2tog, p1. Turn.

Row 7: (RS) Sl 1, k9, ssk, k1. Turn.

Row 8: (WS) Sl 1, p10, p2tog, p1. Turn.

Row 9: (RS) Sl 1, k11, ssk. Turn.

Row 10: (WS) Sl 1, p11, p2tog. Turn. (13 sts remain.)

Work 6 sts; place marker for beg of round.

## Heel gusset

With a free needle (N1), knit remaining 7 heel sts. Continuing with same needle, pick up 10 sts along the side of heel. Pick up and knit 1 st from row below the first instep st to prevent a hole (18 sts on N1). With a free needle (N2), work across 21 instep sts. With free needle (N3), pick up and knit 1 st from row below first heel st to prevent a hole. With same needle, pick up 10 sts along side of heel and work across remaining heel sts (17 sts on N3).

## Shape gusset

Rnd 1 (dec rnd):

N1: Knit to 3 sts from end; k2tog, k1.

N2: (Instep) Work even in ribbing.

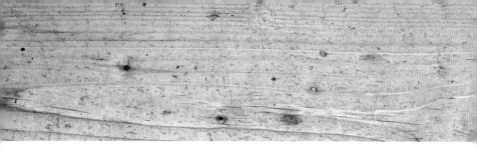

N3: K1, ssk, knit to end.

Rnd 2: Work even, working ribbing on N2 only.

Repeat rnds 1 and 2 until there are 42 sts remaining.

### Foot

Continue working in rnds until foot measures 4" from base of heel. Lengthen or shorten here.

On next rnd, inc 2 sts — 1 st on N1 and 1 st on N2 — complete sts on N3. Place marker for beg of rnd.

### Shape toe

Rnd 1:

N1: (Sole) Work to last 3 sts, k2tog, k1.

N2: (Instep) K1, ssk, work to last 3 sts, k2tog, k1.

N3: (Sole) K1, ssk, complete round.

Rnd 2: Work even.

Repeat rnds 1 and 2 until 28 total sts remain.

Repeat rnd 1 until 12 sts remain (6 instep sts, 6 sole sts).

### Finishing

Work sts on N1. Slip sts from N3 to N1. Holding N1 and N2 together, graft sts using Kitchener stitch (see grafting instructions on page 35). Weave in ends.

# Child's Socks

**Skill level:** Intermediate ●●●○

**Size:** Child shoe size 3

**Finished measurements:**
*Circumference of leg:* 7⅝"
*Length of foot:* 8¼"

**Yarn weight:**

Gauge
32 sts and 40 rows = 4" (10 cm)

Materials
• 1 hank Alpaca Sox by Classic Elite, 60% alpaca, 20% merino wool, 20% nylon (450 yds/100g) in color 1810
• Set of 4 size 2 (2.75 mm) double-pointed needles

Child's socks
Cast on 62 sts loosely.

Divide sts on 3 needles as follows:

Needle 1 (N1): 15 heel sts

Needle 2 (N2): 31 instep sts

Needle 3 (N3): 16 heel sts

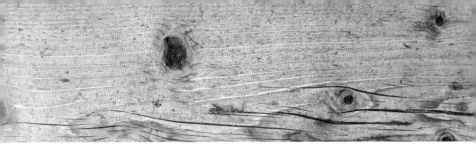

Join and place a marker to indicate beg of round.

## Leg

Work in k1, p1 ribbing for 35 rnds. On next round, complete sts on N2 and stop. (Leg should measure about 4½" from cast-on edge.)

## Heel flap

Slip N3 sts onto N1 (31 sts on needle).

Note: On first row only, k2, M1, complete row (32 sts).

On last row, decrease 1 st (31 sts remain).

With RS facing, work back and forth as follows:

Row 1: *Sl 1 purlwise, k1; repeat from * to end.

Row 2: Sl 1 purlwise, p to end.

Repeat these 2 rows 11 more times (24 rows total).

## Turn heel

Note: Sl 1 = sl 1 purlwise.

Row 1 (RS): K17, ssk, k1. Turn.

Row 2 (WS): Sl 1, p4, p2tog, p1. Turn.

Row 3 (RS): Sl 1, k5, ssk, k1. Turn.

Row 4 (WS): Sl 1, p6, p2tog, p1. Turn.

Row 5 (RS): Sl 1, k7, ssk, k1. Turn.

Row 6 (WS): Sl 1, p8, p2tog, p1. Turn.

Row 7 (RS): Sl 1, k9, ssk, k1. Turn.

Row 8 (WS): Sl 1, p10, p2tog, p1. Turn.

Row 9 (RS): Sl 1, k11, ssk, k1. Turn.

Row 10 (WS): Sl 1, p12, p2tog, p1. Turn.

Row 11 (RS): Sl 1, k13, ssk, k1. Turn.

Row 12 (WS): Sl 1, p14, p2tog, p1. Turn.

www.LoveofKnitting.com

Row 13 (RS): Sl 1, k15, ssk. Turn.

Row 14 (WS): Sl 1, p15, p2tog. Turn. (17 sts remain.)

Work 8 sts; place marker for beg of round.

## Heel gusset

With a free needle (N1), knit remaining 9 heel sts. Continuing with same needle, pick up 12 sts along side of heel.

Pick up and knit 1 st from row below the first instep st to prevent a hole (22 sts on N1).

With a free needle (N2), work across 31 instep sts.

With free needle (N3), pick up and knit 1 st from row below first heel st to prevent a hole. With same needle, pick up 12 sts along side of heel and work across remaining heel sts (21 sts on N3).

## Shape gusset

Rnd 1 (Dec Rnd):

N1: Knit to 3 sts from end; k2tog, k1.

N2: (Instep) Work even in ribbing.

N3: K1, ssk, knit to end.

Rnd 2: Work even, working ribbing on N2 only.

Repeat rnds 1 and 2 until there are 62 sts remaining.

## Foot

Continue working in rnds until foot measures 6⅜" from base of heel. Lengthen or shorten here.

On next rnd, inc 2 sts — 1 st on N1 and 1 st on N2 — complete sts on N3. Place marker for beg of rnd.

## Shape toe

Rnd 1:

N1: (Sole) Work to last 3 sts, k2tog, k1.

N2: (Instep) K1, ssk, work to last 3 sts, k2tog, k1.

N3: (Sole) K1, ssk, complete round.

Rnd 2: Work even.

Repeat rnds 1 and 2 until 40 total sts remain.

Repeat rnd 1 until 16 sts remain (8 instep sts, 8 sole sts).

## Finishing

Work sts on N1. Slip sts from N3 to N1.

Holding N1 and N2 together, graft sts using Kitchener stitch (see grafting instructions on page 35). Weave in ends.

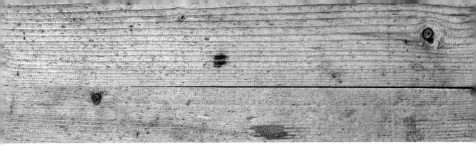

# Women's Socks

**Skill level:** Intermediate ●●●○

**Size:** Women's shoe size to 10

**Finished measurements:**
*Circumference of leg:* 8⅛"
*Length of foot:* 10"

**Yarn weight:**

## Gauge
30 sts and 38 rows = 4" (10 cm)

## Materials
- 1 skein Heritage Solids by Cascade Yarns, 75% Merino Superwash, 25% nylon (437 yds/100g) in color 5607
- Set of 4 size 2 (2.75mm) double-pointed needles

## Stitch pattern
C4B (cable 4 back):

Slip next 2 sts onto cable needle and hold at back of work; knit next 2 sts from left needle; knit sts from cable needle.

## Cable pattern
Rows 1, 2, 4, 5, 6, and 8–12: *P1, k4, p1; repeat from * to end of rnd.

Rows 3 and 7: *P1, C4B, p1; repeat from * to end of rnd.

## Women's socks
Cast on 60 sts loosely.

Divide sts on 3 needles as follows:

Needle 1 (N1): 18 heel sts

Needle 2 (N2): 30 instep sts

Needle 3 (N3): 12 heel sts

Join and place a marker to indicate beg of round.

### Leg
Work in cable patt for 79 rnds. On next round, complete sts on N2 and stop. (Leg should measure about 8" from cast-on edge.)

### Heel flap
Slip N3 sts onto N1 (30 sts on needle).

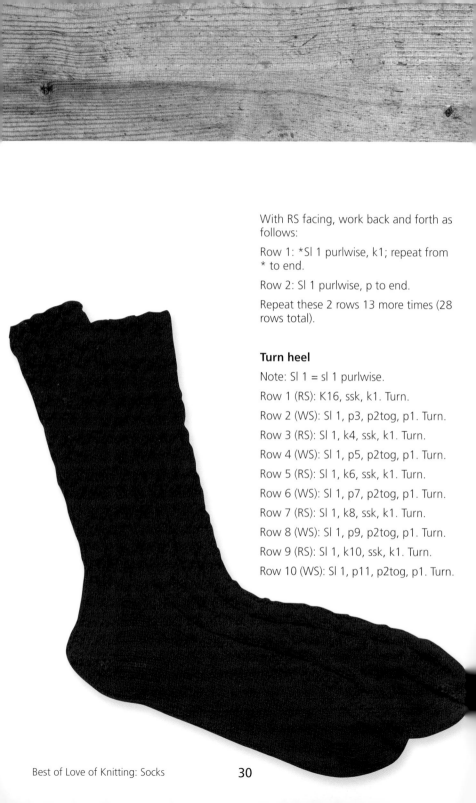

With RS facing, work back and forth as follows:

Row 1: *Sl 1 purlwise, k1; repeat from * to end.

Row 2: Sl 1 purlwise, p to end.

Repeat these 2 rows 13 more times (28 rows total).

**Turn heel**

Note: Sl 1 = sl 1 purlwise.

Row 1 (RS): K16, ssk, k1. Turn.

Row 2 (WS): Sl 1, p3, p2tog, p1. Turn.

Row 3 (RS): Sl 1, k4, ssk, k1. Turn.

Row 4 (WS): Sl 1, p5, p2tog, p1. Turn.

Row 5 (RS): Sl 1, k6, ssk, k1. Turn.

Row 6 (WS): Sl 1, p7, p2tog, p1. Turn.

Row 7 (RS): Sl 1, k8, ssk, k1. Turn.

Row 8 (WS): Sl 1, p9, p2tog, p1. Turn.

Row 9 (RS): Sl 1, k10, ssk, k1. Turn.

Row 10 (WS): Sl 1, p11, p2tog, p1. Turn.

Row 11 (RS): Sl 1, k12, ssk, k1. Turn.

Row 12 (WS): Sl 1, p13, p2tog, p1. Turn.

Row 13 (RS): Sl 1, k14, ssk. Turn.

Row 14 (WS): Sl 1, p14, p2tog. Turn. (16 sts remain.)

Work 8 sts; place marker for beg of round.

### Heel gusset

With a free needle (N1), knit remaining 8 heel sts. Continuing with same needle, pick up 14 sts along side of heel.

Pick up and knit 1 st from row below the first instep st to prevent a hole (23 sts on N1).

With a free needle (N2), work across 30 instep sts.

With a free needle (N3), pick up and knit 1 st from row below first heel st to prevent a hole. With same needle, pick up 14 sts along side of heel and work across remaining heel sts (23 sts on N3).

### Shape gusset

Rnd 1 (dec rnd):

N1: Knit to 3 sts from end; k2tog, k1.

N2: (Instep) Work even in cable patt.

N3: K1, ssk, knit to end.

Rnd 2: Work even, continuing cable patt on N2 only.

Repeat rnds 1 and 2 until there are 60 sts remaining.

### Foot

Continue working in rnds until foot measures 8" from base of heel. Lengthen or shorten here.

### Shape toe

Rnd 1:

N1: (Sole) Knit to last 3 sts, k2tog, k1.

N2: (Instep) K1, ssk, knit to last 3 sts, k2tog, k1.

N3: (Sole) K1, ssk, complete round.

Rnd 2: Knit.

Repeat rnds 1 and 2 until 36 total sts remain.

Repeat rnd 1 until 12 sts remain (6 instep sts, 6 sole sts).

## Finishing

Work sts on N1. Slip sts from N3 to N1. Holding N1 and N2 together, graft sts using Kitchener stitch (see grafting instructions on page 35). Weave in ends.

# Men's Socks

**Skill level:** Intermediate ●●●○

**Size:** Men's size 10–13

**Finished measurements:**
*Circumference of leg:* 8⅞"
*Length of foot:* 11"

**Yarn weight:**

## Gauge
30 sts and 42 rows = 4" (10 cm)

## Materials
- 2 skeins Regia, 75% Superwash wool, 25% polyamide (130 yds/50g) in color 5563
- Set of 4 size 2 (2.75 mm) double-pointed needles

## Men's socks
Cast on 66 sts loosely.

Divide sts on 3 needles as follows:

Needle 1 (N1): 16 heel sts

Needle 2 (N2): 33 instep sts

Needle 3 (N3): 17 heel sts

Join and place a marker to indicate beg of round.

## Leg
Work in K2, p1 ribbing for 94 rnds. On next round, complete sts on N2 and stop. (Leg should measure about 9" from cast-on edge.)

## Heel flap
Slip N3 sts onto N1 (33 sts on needle).

Note: On first row only, work 2 sts in pat st, M1, complete row (34 sts).

On last row, decrease 1 st (33 sts remain).

With RS facing, work back and forth as follows:

Row 1: *Sl 1 purlwise, k1; repeat from * to end.

Row 2: Sl 1 purlwise, p to end.

Repeat these 2 rows 16 more times (34 rows total).

## Turn heel
Note: Sl 1 = sl 1 purlwise.

Row 1 (RS): K18, ssk, k1. Turn.

Row 2 (WS): Sl 1, p4, p2tog, p1. Turn.

Row 3 (RS): Sl 1, k5, ssk, k1. Turn.

Row 4 (WS): Sl 1, p6, p2tog, p1. Turn.

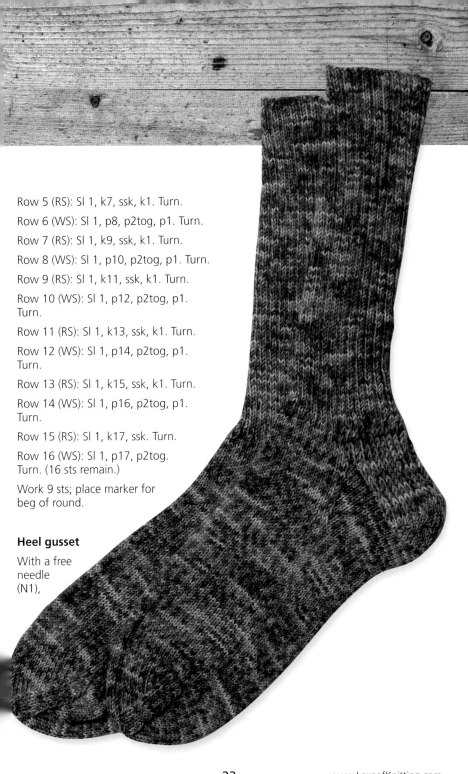

Row 5 (RS): Sl 1, k7, ssk, k1. Turn.

Row 6 (WS): Sl 1, p8, p2tog, p1. Turn.

Row 7 (RS): Sl 1, k9, ssk, k1. Turn.

Row 8 (WS): Sl 1, p10, p2tog, p1. Turn.

Row 9 (RS): Sl 1, k11, ssk, k1. Turn.

Row 10 (WS): Sl 1, p12, p2tog, p1.
Turn.

Row 11 (RS): Sl 1, k13, ssk, k1. Turn.

Row 12 (WS): Sl 1, p14, p2tog, p1.
Turn.

Row 13 (RS): Sl 1, k15, ssk, k1. Turn.

Row 14 (WS): Sl 1, p16, p2tog, p1.
Turn.

Row 15 (RS): Sl 1, k17, ssk. Turn.

Row 16 (WS): Sl 1, p17, p2tog.
Turn. (16 sts remain.)

Work 9 sts; place marker for
beg of round.

**Heel gusset**

With a free
needle
(N1),

knit remaining 10 heel sts. Continuing with same needle, pick up 17 sts along side of heel.

Pick up and knit 1 st from row below the first instep st to prevent a hole (28 sts on N1).

With a free needle (N2), work across 33 instep sts.

With a free needle (N3), pick up and knit 1 st from row below first heel st to prevent a hole. With same needle, pick up 17 sts along side of heel and work across remaining heel sts (27 sts on N3).

### Shape gusset

Rnd 1 (dec rnd):

N1: Knit to 3 sts from end; k2tog, k1.

N2: (Instep) Work even in k2, p1 rib.

N3: K1, ssk, knit to end.

Rnd 2: Work even, continuing rib pattern on N2 only.

Repeat rnds 1 and 2 until there are 66 sts remaining.

### Foot

Continue working in rnds until foot measures 9" from base of heel.

Lengthen or shorten here.

On next rnd, inc 2 sts — 1 st on N1 and 1 st on N2 — complete sts on N3. Place marker for beg of rnd.

### Shape Toe

Rnd 1:

N1: (Sole) Knit to last 3 sts, k2tog, k1.

N2: (Instep) K1, ssk, knit to last 3 sts, k2tog, k1.

N3: (Sole) K1, ssk, complete round.

Rnd 2: Knit.

Repeat rnds 1 and 2 until 40 total sts remain.

Repeat rnd 1 until 12 sts remain (6 instep sts, 6 sole sts).

## Finishing

Work sts on N1. Slip sts from N3 to N1.

Holding N1 and N2 together, graft sts using Kitchener stitch (see grafting instructions on page 35).

Weave in ends. ▣

# Grafting or Kitchener stitch

*Use a blunt-tipped yarn needle to join two pieces of knitting that have not been bound off. Grafting creates an invisible join with stitches that exactly match the knitted stitches. Use this technique to finish all of the socks.*

**1.** Arrange two pieces of knitting with same number of stitches on each needle and wrong sides facing. Thread the tail from the back piece through yarn needle. Insert yarn needle as if to purl in first stitch on front needle. Leave stitch on needle (photo A).

A

**B**

*Note: We used a contrasting yarn in our sample to show the stitches better. Use matching yarn when grafting two pieces together.*

**2.** Insert yarn needle through first stitch on back needle as if to knit. Leave stitch on needle (photo B).

**3.** Bring yarn needle through first stitch on front needle as if to knit and slip stitch off needle. Bring yarn needle through next front stitch as if to purl and leave stitch on needle (photo C).

**C**

**4.** Bring yarn needle through first stitch on back needle as if to purl and slip stitch off needle. Bring yarn needle through next back stitch as if to knit and leave stitch on needle (photo D).

**5.** Repeat steps 3 and 4 until no stitches remain on needles. Adjust tension of the stitches as you go to make them match the knitted stitches (photo E).

# Basic knitting instructions

## Twisted loop cast on

The twisted loop cast on is an easy method that will produce a soft, elastic edge. It is a great choice for adding on stitches or when knitting lace.

**1** Make a slip knot with a tail long enough to cast on required number of stitches (about ½" per stitch); place slip knot on needle. Holding needle and yarn tail from ball in right hand, wrap yarn from back to front around left thumb; hold tail with your fingers (photo A).

**2** Bring needle from bottom to top through loop of yarn on thumb (photo B).

**3** Slide loop off thumb and pull on yarn tail to tighten loop on needle (photo C).

**4** Repeat steps 2 and 3 to cast on required number of stitches.

**Knit smart™** If your cast-on stitches are too tight, use a needle one or two sizes larger than the pattern calls for. Switch back to correct needle size before you begin to knit.

# Knitted cast on

The knitted cast on method produces a loose, soft edge. This would not be a good choice for a garment with a ribbed edge, as it will look sloppy.

**1** Make a slip knot, leaving a short tail (at least 4"); place slip knot on left needle.

**2** Insert tip of right needle from left to right through the loop. Tip of right needle will be behind left needle (photo A).

**3** Wrap yarn from back to front over right needle, then down between the two needles (photo B).

**4** Bring tip of right needle forward through stitch on left needle, keeping wrapped yarn on right needle. Wrapped yarn forms a new stitch on right needle (photo C).

**5** Insert left needle from right to left through loop on right needle (photo D).

**6** Remove right needle from loop and gently tighten stitch on left needle (photo E).

**7** Repeat steps 2–6 to cast on required number of stitches.

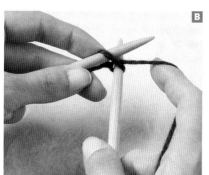

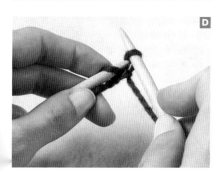

## Knit stitch

**1** Hold needle with stitches in left hand; hold empty needle in right hand. Insert tip of right needle from left to right into front of stitch on left needle. Tip of right needle will be behind left needle (photo A).

**2** Wrap yarn from back to front over right needle, then down between the two needles (photo B).

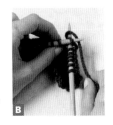

**3** Bring tip of right needle forward through stitch on left needle, keeping wrapped yarn on right needle. Wrapped yarn forms a new stitch on right needle (photo C).

**4** Slide right needle to the right, slipping stitch off left needle. Continue in same manner to the end of the row (photo D).

## Purl stitch

**1** Hold needle with stitches in left hand; hold empty needle in right hand. Insert tip of right needle from right to left into front of stitch on left needle. Yarn and right needle will be in front of left needle (photo A).

**2** Wrap yarn from right to left around right needle (photo B).

**3** Bring tip of right needle backward through stitch on left needle, keeping wrapped yarn on right needle. Wrapped yarn forms a new stitch on right needle (photo C).

**4** Slide right needle to the right, slipping stitch off left needle. Continue in same manner to the end of the row (photo D).

## Decrease: knit 2 together (k2tog)

**1** At point of decrease, insert right needle from left to right through two stitches (photo A).

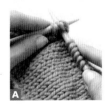

**2** Wrap yarn from back to front around right needle; bring right needle forward through both stitches on left needle. Wrapped yarn forms stitch on right needle (photo B).

**3** Slide right needle to the right, slipping stitches off left needle. You have decreased one stitch (photo C).

**4** Decrease will slant toward the right (photo D).

## Decrease: slip, slip, knit (ssk)

**1** At point of decrease, slip two stitches knitwise, one at a time, onto right needle. Insert left needle from left to right through front of the two slipped stitches on right needle (photo A).

**2** Wrap yarn from back to front around right needle; bring right needle forward through both stitches on left needle. Wrapped yarn forms stitch on right needle (photo B).

**3** Slide right needle to the right, slipping stitches off left needle. You have decreased one stitch (photo C).

**4** Decrease will slant toward the left (photo D).

## Increase: knit in the front and back (k1 f&b or kfb)

**1** At point of increase, knit stitch, but do not remove stitch from left needle (photo A).

**2** Insert tip of right needle from right to left through back of same loop on left needle. Tip of right needle will be behind left needle (photo B).

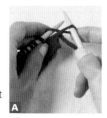

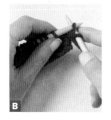

**3** Wrap yarn from back to front around right needle; bring right needle forward through stitch on left needle, keeping wrapped yarn on right needle. There are now two stitches on right needle (photo C).

**4** Slide right needle to the right, slipping stitch off left needle. You have increased one stitch (photo D).

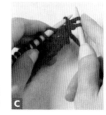

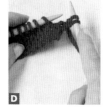

## Grafting or Kitchener stitch

**1** Arrange two pieces of knitting with same number of stitches on each needle and wrong sides facing. Thread the tail from the back piece through yarn needle. Insert yarn needle as if to purl in first stitch on front needle. Leave stitch on needle (photo A).

**2** Insert yarn needle through first stitch on back needle as if to knit. Leave stitch on needle (photo B).

**3** Bring yarn needle through first stitch on front needle as if to knit and slip stitch off needle. Bring yarn needle through next

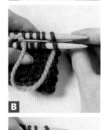

front stitch as if to purl and leave stitch on needle (photo C).

**4** Bring yarn needle through first stitch on back needle as if to purl and slip stitch off needle. Bring yarn needle through next back stitch as if to knit and leave stitch on needle (photo D).

**5** Repeat steps 3 and 4 until no stitches remain on needles. Adjust tension of the stitches as you go to make them match the knitted stitches (photo E).

**Note:** We used a contrasting yarn in our sample to show the stitches better. Use matching yarn when grafting two pieces together.

# Binding off

**1** Knit first two stitches from left needle (photo A).

**2** Insert left needle from left to right into front of first stitch on right needle. Lift first stitch over second stitch and over end of right needle (photo B).

**3** Slip left needle out of stitch and let it drop (photo C). (One stitch remains on right needle.)

**4** Knit next stitch from left needle and repeat the last two steps. Continue across row until there are no stitches on left needle and one stitch remains on right needle (photo D).

**5** Cut yarn, leaving at least a 4" tail. Pull end of yarn through loop of last stitch (photo E).

**6** Pull on yarn tail to tighten the loop (photo F).

## Standard yarn weight system

| Yarn weight symbol and category names | Lace (0) | Super Fine (1) | Fine (2) | Light (3) | Medium (4) | Bulky (5) | Super Bulky (6) |
|---|---|---|---|---|---|---|---|
| Type of yarns in category | Fingering, 10 count, crochet thread | Sock, Fingering, Baby | Sport, Baby | DK, Light Worsted | Worsted, Afghan, Aran | Chunky, Craft, Rug | Bulky Roving |
| Knit gauge range* in stockinette stitch to 4 inches | 33–40** sts | 27–32 sts | 23–26 sts | 21–24 sts | 16–20 sts | 12–15 sts | 6–11 st |
| Recommended needle in mm and metric size range | 1.5–2.25 mm | 2.25–3.25 mm | 3.25–3.75 mm | 3.75–4.5 mm | 4.5–5.5 mm | 5.5–8 mm | 8 mm and larger |
| Recommended needle in U.S. size range | 000 to 1 | 1 to 3 | 3 to 5 | 5 to 7 | 7 to 9 | 9 to 11 | 11 and larger |
| Crochet gauge* ranges in single crochet to 4 inches | 32–42 double crochets** | 21–32 sts | 16–20 sts | 12–17 sts | 11–14 sts | 8–11 sts | 5–9 sts |
| Recommended hook in metric size range | Steel*** 1.6–1.4mm Regular hook 2.25 mm | 2.25–3.5 mm | 3.5–4.5 mm | 4.5–5.5 mm | 5.5–6.5 mm | 6.5–9 mm | 9mm and larger |
| Recommended hook in U.S. size range | Steel*** 6, 7, 8 Regular hook B–1 | B–1 to E–4 | E–4 to 7 | 7 to I–9 | I–9 to K–10 1/2 | K–10 1/2 to M–13 | M–13 and larger |

* These are guidelines only: They reflect the most commonly used gauges and needle or hook sizes for specific yarn categories.

** Lace weight yarns are usually knitted or crocheted on larger needles and hooks to create lacy, openwork patterns. Accordingly, a gauge range is difficult to determine. Always follow the gauge stated in your pattern.

*** Steel crochet hooks are sized differently from regular hooks — the higher the number, the smaller the hook, which is the reverse of regular hook sizing.

A Standard & Guidelines booklet from the Craft Yarn Council of America is available at www.craftyarncouncil.com/standards.html. Click on the "Downloadable Guidelines PDF" link on the left side of the page.

# Skill levels for knitting

●○○○ **Beginner** Projects for first-time knitters using basic knit and purl stitches. Minimal shaping.

●●○○ **Easy** Projects using basic stitches, repetitive stitch patterns, simple color changes, and simple shaping and finishing.

●●●○ **Intermediate** Projects with a variety of stitches, such as basic cables and lace, simple intarsia, double-pointed needles and knitting-in-the-round needle techniques, mid-level shaping and finishing.

●●●● **Experienced** Projects using advanced techniques and stitches, such as short rows, Fair Isle, more intricate intarsia, cables, lace patterns, and numerous color changes.

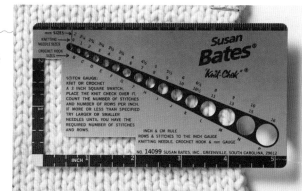

## Check your gauge

For best results, always take time to check your gauge. Using the same needles and yarn you will use for your project, knit a swatch that is about 5" (12.5 cm) square. Count the number of stitches and rows in 4". If you have more rows or stitches than indicated in your pattern, try larger needles and knit another swatch. If you have fewer rows or stitches than indicated, make another swatch using smaller needles. Continue this process until your swatch matches the numbers given in your pattern. Although this seems tedious, it is worth the time to increase the accuracy of the finished size of your project. A gauge tool, such as the one shown, can aid in counting stitches and rows.

www.LoveofKnitting.com

## Standard knitting abbreviations

**\*** repeat starting point (repeat from \*)

**\*\*** repeat all instructions between asterisks

**( )** alternate measurements and/or work instructions in parentheses in place directed

**[ ]** work instructions in brackets a specified number of times

**approx** approximately

**beg** beginning; begin, begins

**bet** between

**BO** bind off

**BOR** beginning of row or round

**C2B** slip 1 st to cable needle and hold in back, k1, k1 from cable needle

**C2F** slip 1 st to cable needle and hold in front, k1, k1 from cable needle

**C4B** slip 2 sts to cable needle and hold in back, k2, k2 from cable needle

**C4F** slip 2 sts to cable needle and hold in front, k2, k2 from cable needle

**CC** contrasting color

**cdd** centered double decrease; sl 2 tog, k1, pass the slipped stitches over (together)

**cm** centimeter(s)

**cn** cable needle

**CO** cast on

**cont** continue(s); continuing

**dec(s)** decrease(s); decreasing

**DPN** double-pointed needles

**EOR** every other row

**foll** following; follows

**g** gram(s)

**inc** increase(s); increasing

**k** knit

**kfb/k1f&b** knit into front and back of same stitch

**k1 tbl** knit 1 through the back loop

**k2tog** knit two stitches together

**k2tog tbl** knit 2 stitches together through the back loops

**k3tog** knit 3 stitches together

**kwise** knitwise

**LC** left cross

**LH** left hand

**m(s)** marker(s)

**MC** main color

**mm** millimeter(s)

**M1/M1L** (make 1 left): An increase. From the front, lift loop between stitches with left needle, knit into back of loop.

**M1p/M1pL** (make 1 purl left): Pick up bar between needles with left needle from front to back. Purl through back loop.

**M1PR**  (make 1 purl right): Pick up bar between needles with left needle from back to front. Purl.

**M1R**  (make 1 right): An increase. From the back, lift loop between stitches with left needle, knit into front of loop.

**oz**  ounce(s)

**p**  purl

**p1f&b**  purl into front and back of same stitch

**p2tog**  purl 2 stitches together

**pat(s)**  pattern(s)

**pm**  place marker

**psso**  pass slipped stitch over

**p2sso**  pass two slipped stitches over

**PU**  pick up and knit stitches with RS facing

**pwise**  purlwise

**RC**  right cross

**rem**  remain(s); remaining

**rep**  repeat; repeating

**rev St st**  reverse stockinette stitch

**RH**  right hand

**rib**  ribbing

**rnd(s)**  round(s)

**RS**  right side

**sk**  skip

**skp**  slip, knit, pass stitch over (decrease)

**sk2p/sl1-k2tog-psso**
slip 1, knit 2 together, pass slip stitch over the knit 2 together — 2 stitch decrease

**sl**  slip

**sl 1k**  slip 1 knitwise

**sl 1p**  slip 1 purlwise

**sl 2**  slip 2 together

**sl 2-k1-psso/sl 2tog-k1-p2sso**  slip 2 together, knit 1, pass 2 slipped sts over — 2 stitch decrease

**sl st**  slip stitch (sl 1 st pwise unless otherwise indicated)

**ssk**  slip 1 knitwise, slip 1 kwise, k2 sl sts tog tbl (decrease)

**SSK-P**  ssk, slip st back to LH needle, pass second st on LH needle over last st, slip st back to RH needle

**ssp**  slip 1 kwise, slip 1 kwise, p2 sl sts tog tbl (decrease)

**st(s)**  stitch(es)

**St st**  stockinette stitch

**T2B**  slip 1 st to cable needle and hold in back, k1, p1 from cable needle

**T2F**  slip 1 st to cable needle and hold in front, p1, k1 from cable needle

**tbl**  through back loop

**tog**  together

**WS**  wrong side

**wyb**  with yarn in back

**wyf**  with yarn in front

**yd(s)**  yard(s)

**yo**  yarn over

**yo2**  yarn over twice

# Love of knitting

**LEISURE ARTS**
*the art of everyday living*
www.leisurearts.com

**LOVE OF KNITTING EDITORIAL STAFF**
**Editor-in-Chief:** Jennifer Burt
**Art Director:** Kathy Locke
**Associate Editor:** Sarah Nagel
**Technical Editor:** Amy Polcyn
**Graphic Designer:** Danielle Fay
**Illustrator:** Marla Stefanelli
**Photography:** J.C. Leacock,
Mellisa Karlin Mahoney

**Publisher:** Lisa O'Bryan
**Advertising Sales:** Megan Smith

**CREATIVE CRAFTS GROUP, LLC**
**President and CEO:** Stephen J. Kent
**VP/Group Publisher:** Tina Battock
**Chief Financial Officer:** Mark F. Arnett
**President, Book Publishing:** Budge Wallis
**Controller:** Jordan Bohrer
**VP/Publishing Director:** Joel P. Toner
**VP/Production:** Barbara Schmitz
**VP/Consumer Marketing and Group Marketing
Director:** Nicole McGuire

**LEISURE ARTS EDITORIAL STAFF**
**Vice President of Editorial:** Susan White Sullivan
**Special Projects Director:** Susan Frantz Wiles
**Director of E-Commerce and Prepress Services:**
Mark Hawkins
**Creative Art Director:** Katherine Laughlin
**Imaging Technician:** Stephanie Johnson
**Prepress Technician:** Janie Marie Wright
**Manager of E-Commerce:** Robert Young

**LEISURE ARTS BUSINESS STAFF**
**President and Chief Executive Officer:** Rick Barton
**Vice President of Finance:** Laticia Mull Dittrich
**Director of Corporate Planning:** Anne Martin
**National Sales Director:** Martha Adams
**Information Technology Director:** Brian Roden
**Controller:** Francis Caple
**Vice President of Operations:** Jim Dittrich
**Retail Customer Service Manager:** Stan Raynor
**Vice President of Purchasing:** Fred F. Pruss

We have made every effort to ensure that these
instructions are accurate and complete. We cannot,
however, be responsible for human error, typographical
mistakes, or variations in individual work.

Published by Leisure Arts, Inc., 5701 Ranch Drive, Little
Rock, Arkansas 72223-9633, leisurearts.com.
Made in China.
ISBN-13: 978-1-4647-0867-1

LIKE US, FOLLOW US, PIN US: